some of our poems

2023

Denholme Scribes

Denholme Scribes

copyright

Copyright © 2023 by Denholme Scribes
All rights reserved.
No part of this book may be reproduced in any form or by any electronic or mechanical means, including information storage and retrieval systems, without written permission from the author, except for the use of brief quotations in a book review.

Cover Art by http://www.fiverr.com/designrans
Cover Illustration by Sheila Gardner

faded blooms by tina watkin

Here we sit awaiting sales
And feeling so dejected.
We're in a corner hidden away,
No way to be detected.

Who will paid attention now?
We wait with withered shoots
For somebody to come along
And sprucen up our roots.

We've been removed from off the shelf
We're literally dying of thirst
Back of the store no one can see,
Surely that is worst.

They'll pass us by not turn an eye
Because we have been caged
To go onto the compost heap
We're feeling so enraged.

Quite neglected, undetected,
Now wouldn't you really think
That some kind soul would notice us
And give us all a drink.

But every one's so busy
No time for dying blooms
To rescue us from such a fate
To glorify their rooms.

Yet wait, Tina has noticed us
And gives her inspection
"Don't worry guys, I'll buy you",
So here's to resurrection.

We're in her garden recovering
She forked out 40p that day
And now she's reaped the riches
Of our brilliant display.

So don't ignore, when in a store
Things which don't quite pass the test.
Those things which look more jaded
Can be better than the best.

on the straight by rose johnson

A stealthy mover on this silent passage
Parting the calm with rippled arrow
And purring rhythmic chug as friend
A distant bird sings a capella

Its painted wooden structure fore to aft
Sails the straight with house on back
As slow as a snail carving watery track
And loyal path beside

Fresh paint adorns its windowed side
By painter's hand with expertise
Of floral motif and patterned line
Like oils to canvas

With stern to guide it on its way
At graceful pace to watch awhile
The passing scene to scrutinise
Of country and of town

Ahead the gates of sturdy lock
where calm meets turbulence
And the aqueous straight must even up
To different level

No longer impelled by equine power
And rarely used for mainstay trade
Just aggregate and people pleasure
But highly prized by one and all

greeting card rhymes
by julie pryke

Illness
We are sorry to hear that you're ill,
You'll have to keep taking the pill,
The lump on your head
Is what keeps you in bed,
But the shrieking is really too shrill!

Bereavement
Oh no! Your frog has just died,
I bet you just sat down and cried,
But with potatoes or rice,
It really tastes nice -
And you could have it roasted or fried.

New job, old joke!
So, Fred has just started school,
We hope that he follows the rule,
He mustn't be late,
Or run out the gate,
The pupils will think he's a fool.

Holidays
Enjoy your exotic holiday,
We'll guard your house whilst you're away,
But if you're away too long,
And find your favourite things are gone...
"It wasn't us!" That's what we'll say.

lest we forget by sheila kendall

Like giant birds of prey they took to the sky
Emptying their payload from way up on high
So what if it's Dresden, Berlin or Cologne
Tell them of London, of England, of home.

Winging their way oe'r land, sea and shore
Ensuring your freedom they gave of their all.

Forget all your preaching now years are long gone
Objections are easy once deeds have been done
Remember instead their freedom, their youth
Gone in six years as they fought for you
Enter their names in the log books of pride
To tell them, at last, you are on their side.

swimming with whales
by julie pryke

People want to swim with sharks,
But always in a cage.

They want to swim with dolphins,
Though never in a rage.

But no-one wants to swim with whales...
... since Jonah!

no flies on me by rose johnson

What is it that makes these creatures so hated
With an image in life that's always berated
Could it be their allure to the dung and decay
Where their babies are born, what more can one say
And after to settle on sugar and butter
Then vomit and liquefy food for their supper
Their ability to taste is inbuilt in their feet
They can walk upside down as well as excrete
So mind your heads that's a warning to you
You could find yourselves all covered in poo
Their probing proboscis persistently delve
Showing ample dare and considerable nerve
Their acute reactions and speedy avoidance
Cause so many, significant annoyance
With compound eyes they're bound to win
Their battles with swats, firmly hands down
Without the fly we would lose such a lot
So many kinds of beauties with colours to spot
As pollinators they're ace, akin to the bee
They're food for the frog and the spider you see
The gardeners love them for aphids they eat

Their indulgence in pests is real tough to beat
But sadly the diptera are in steady decline
Their extinction would mean the end of the line
There's no flies on me and I hope that I'm wrong
And we would no more sing life's glorious song

silence by sheila kendall

Sometimes I yearn for silence
Just a quiet place to dream
I cannot wait with patience
To find that life serene.

Must I look toward the stars
In their icy, bright profusion
Leave behind my life's confusion
Shake away my earthly garb.

My time has come, I dare not dally
I rush to meet my solitude
To walk along my hidden valley
And dream my dreams in plenitude.

penistone hill by rose johnson

From bumpy stony track to peak the summit
No ledges, drops from which to plummet
A quarried mound that boasts sweet heather
Loyal and strong despite the weather

The climb to top, a meagre stroll
But views abound, sights to extol
Bilberries aplenty on summer day
Rich pickings from a lush array

On one grey stone, a single rose is laid
Where envied views boast hills of jade
In memory of a beloved view
Recalled by one faithful and true

Down slopy rubble on rugged track
A tarn exists amid the crags
A mirrored well by fallen sky
For calm reflection to stay awhile

And on to sepulchred random rock
Sculptured by time, turn back the clock
Grand memories of those since gone
Each tilted stone bears one loved name

Proud Penistone portal to the way
Not much to see, I hear you say
But look awhile on peaty ground
Penistone hill, not just a mound

the new frock by julie pryke

"Do you like my frock?" said Snow White to Doc,

"It looks a bit lumpy I think!" said Grumpy,

"Was it a cheapy?" said the one who was Sleepy,

"I hope it weren't ropey, I'm worried" said Dopey,

"You look like a rascal" said the young one called Bashful,

"I'm still feeling queasy, I've a cold!" said our Sneezy,

"It looks really snappy, I promise!" said Happy,

"I'm glad it's alright!" said the maid called Snow White.

sunday morning wake up call (an alliteration exercise) by tina watkin

Barry with his baton bumps up louder on the beat.
Sam strikes sharp upon his cymbals waking up the street.

Trevor toots his trumpet attempting to stay in time
As Liz loses her pages and limps lazily out of line.

Denis is doddering, dumping down his drum.
Tom's ears are trembling trying to shield the thrum.

Tony trumps on his tuba, thinks he can't be heard.
Xavier on a xylophone explains that's quite absurd.

Eric's euphonium is equally far too loud.
Causing children crying, congregating in the crowd.

Bazil blowing his bassoon is dribbling on his suit,
Whilst Frances in floral frock feels famous on the flute.

Bernard brushes onward behaving like a prat,
As Betty bravely battles on, no idea where she's at.

You see, she's new and forgot to bring her instrument
    along
So now she's going psychic. She's been told to sing a
    song.

Harry's got entangled, contorted in his Horn.
Basil's blaming his parents, wishing he'd never been
    born

Because everyone burst out laughing, thinking it a joke,
First time his puck plucked three guitar strings broke.

Clara's Clarinet's churns out notes not yet written,
Scaring 'Little Samson', my newly acquired kitten,

Heard every week by walkers, giving them a rousing
    hand.
Ducking back under my duvet, I curse the ... Sunday
    Morning Band.

THIS WAS *the Denholme Boys Brigade Band in the 1980's.*

state of the art by rose johnson

I came along with high expectations
Dashed hopes of grandeur, instead defacement
A ruined mass of fallen structure
Displaced gray stones in random stature

A mist alighted like a screen
A passing shroud that blurred the scene
And when it lifted a man I saw
Standing by what seemed a door

With hand he beckoned fervently
Responding, I sensed his urgency
I entered the ruins like a ghost
And followed with awe my new found host

He cast my mind back to an age
Of decadence, richness, hard to gauge
My eyes receptive I was beginning to see
Its many rooms, now clear to me

I stepped into a hall with floors of marble
And sweeping staircase, a sight to to marvel
A gallery of oils adorned the wall
The face of my guide appeared in them all

He smiled at me when I gasped in wonder
At the treasures in view on which to ponder
Porcelain, tapestry, it had the lot
Even a dance floor for pavane and gavotte

Four poster beds with embroidered drapes
The musty smell was hard to take
From mullioned window I glimpsed the lake
With swans and ducks, I make no mistake

Manicured lawns and statuettes
Embraced the borders like silhouettes
Reflecting the atmosphere of this time
A far away bell had started to chime

What happened here I asked the man
Squandered by me and the rest of the clan
We waged a bet and sadly lost
It all went at such great cost

The toll of the bell was getting louder
He turned to go, he was losing his power
Fast fading before my very eyes
Now in the ruins and the demise

I browse the toppled masonry once grand
I sense his smile, his presence, his waving hand
Once garden, in place the moss and ivy grow
With sad reflection I turn to go.

have you got time to help with my rhyme?
by julie pryke

"Have you got time to help with my rhyme?"
Said the cat to the mouse, as he peeped in her house.
"I'm sorry, oh no! I just have to go!"
Said the mouse to the cat, as she hid in a hat.

"Have you got time to help with my rhyme?"
Said the cat to the cow as it stood by the plough,
"I'm sorry, oh no! I just have to go"
Said the cow to the cat, "I've got no time to chat!"

"Have you got time to help with my rhyme?"
Said the cat to the bird, who thought it absurd,
"I'm sorry, oh no! I just have to go"
Said the bird to the cat, as it munched on a gnat!

"Have you got time to help with my rhyme?"
Said the cat to the frog as it sat on a log.
"I'm sorry, oh no! I just have to go"
Said the frog to the cat, as it jumped away, splat!

"Have you got time to help with my rhyme?
Said the cat to the flea as he scratched it with glee
The flea said "Oh yes", as he made quite a mess,
Sucking blood from the poor old cat's knee.

reaping the benefit by rose johnson

The midday sun blazed on the field
Where parched crops refused to yield
A barren sprawl that awaits cool rain
To yet again produce the grain

Trespassing a way upon this land
A shrewd eyed man, detector in hand
And knapsack wobbling on his back
As yet no find to make a stack

The time went by upon this plot
The dying day no longer hot
Shadows spread across the ground
The elusive treasure still not found

The fading sun took pity on the gent
A dying ray of amber hope was sent
It alighted on a beer can ring
And turned it into gold from tin

It nestled amid a shrivelled vine
The sun had given it a lustrous shine
The man could not believe his luck
He dropped to his knees and picked it up

He cast the detector to one side
His skyward glance was gratified
The precious gift was in his hand
A ring of gold, an eternity band.

The moon now gazed from obscure sky
On table top it did espy
The golden ring next to the bed
And sleeping man in his homestead

Its lunar rays cast light from dark
To sit on the ring and leave its mark
From gold to tin it was transformed
The ring to beer pull newly formed

lost souls by dawn stott

Wind brushes against my solemn face
As I watch and stare at the empty space
No longer near, now so far away
How life can change in just one day
Settled now, the calm after the raging storm
I watch the rise of a reluctant dawn
My heart is heavy and enormously cold
As I think of the seventeen lost souls
To touch, to feel just one more time
The man, a father, I used to call mine
The debris of the night's long tempest
Lies lifeless and wasted, now at rest
A tear trickles down my fervent cheek
I walk to the edge and gently weep
The only place to feel you now is in my heart
I will wait patiently for my life to restart
A simple flower is all I can send
To my lover, my partner my lifelong friend

flatpack wonder by rose johnson

Procured from mega shop, a straight-lined box amid a cardboard wall
Where jigsaw chattels rise above the queues of flatbed wheelies
And underarm catalogues patterned with an iconic list of what they are
When the blocks are sequenced and affixed with laborious strife
A transformation takes place that gives the pack new form herewith
Long live the flat pack table and its tedious sway in frail chipboard
Seated upon upon a quartet of nailed on props that creak objection
It takes its varnished place in harmony with four bolted chairs that match
And for a while it serves to hold the plates and cutlery just grand
Until the careless etch of scratches weave marring patterns on its top
Forever to remain as though a work of scribbled art and wrinkled mess

No longer wavelets in the soup, a tidal wave is now the norm when the legs teeter
Today the food's aslant and the drinks decide to slide and slither to the floor
The props have given way, they're tired and now submit to glory
And the table returns again to flat pack with eternal gratitude

four ways out by tina watkin

The knife was so sharp
He goaded her once again
Finding out it was.

The cake tempted her.
It only took a minute
The poison didn't.

Wired for sound she lay
Till she dropped the radio
The bath killed her off.

She tried to reverse
The wall never moved at all
Oh dear, two left feet.

she was scared by julie pryke

She had always been into hob-knobbing,
She took up with a young man called Robin,
But she had to admit she was scared.

They went for a walk, her hair bobbing,
And looked at the bank they'd be robbing,
But she had to admit she was scared.

They robbed it next day, her heart throbbing,
When she saw the PC, plod, plod, plodding,
She had to admit she was scared.

Her fingerprints they were swabbing,
Both she and Robin were sobbing,
It was true ...
        she confessed, ...
                she was scared!

out of steam by rose johnson

Powered by vapour and shovelled coal
On levelled tracks to take it to its goal
A mobile kettle seething at its seams
Polished with care, see how it gleams
Smoke billows and rolls out of the stack
Fleetingly turning the cold air black
Pistons, shunts, maintain its motion
Created with hard work and devotion
Large wheels turn with rhythmic clack
Speed near forty, there's no going back
Betwixt towns and cities it's closed the gap
For cargo and people. It's on the last lap.
Proudly it nears its place of arrival
Fine, moulded steel and hard to rival
With a whistle and a shriek and breaks applied
It's a symbol of the past in a place of pride
Buffer upon buffer it remains in its bay
Out of steam and puff until the next day
Now used to remind of an industrial past
A far cry from ones now electrified and fast
This prototype of steam, an engineer's whiz
Remains for all to see and relive.

water: a collection of five poems by julie pryke

the beck by julie pryke

As water trickles from the source
The beck flows rhythmically down the hill.
The Sun's rays, bright shafts,
Causing shadows and highlights.
As the beck glides along its path,
Kingfishers dive, insects hover,
Small birds, swiftly dip, feeding.
It is never still, gracefully it runs,
It ripples over the rocks,
Fashioning mini waterfalls,
Met by the stream.
Met by the stream,
Fashioning mini waterfalls,
It ripples over the rocks,
It is never still, gracefully it runs.
Small birds, swiftly dip, feeding.
Kingfishers dive, insects hover,
As the beck glides along its path.
Causing shadows and highlights,
The Sun's rays, bright shafts.
The beck flows rhythmically down the hill,
As water trickles from the source.

the stream by julie pryke

The stream starts quietly, gently bubbling through the
    gap in the cliff, forcing a passage.
Forging its way, the heavy rain intensifies it.

The start of a waterfall, perhaps, up in the Dales?
But no! It strives to travel further; has an ambition it is
    determined to fulfil.

It stumbles over stones, pebbles worn smooth over time.
it gathers more and more water as it leaps over the bigger
    rocks,
And pushes the simplest path it can find through the
    valley.

It tickles children's feet as they paddle with glee.

As it runs quickly along, it makes its distinctive babbling
    noise.
It follows the same path always unless an intervention is
    made.
It is part of nature, essential clear water: even now it
    holds the power.

Gradually eating away at the bed of the watercourse,
    eroding stones down to sand,

Rejoicing as it gets stronger,
And over the next rocks it forms a pool, anticipating
    future visits from beavers, voles, water-rats.
It is used by cows and sheep to quench their thirst, and
    by dogs to frolic and have fun.

Waterfowl begin to appear, ducks, diving birds, king-
    fishers,
All start to establish themselves,
All celebrate its presence,

Dragonflies breed and hover, laying eggs under the
    water,
Bees tend the growing plant life, small trees develop.
Tadpoles, frogs, toads and small fish miraculously
    appear there, swimming, seeking protection, food,
    and shelter,
As they go on life's journey.

A heron visits and hides in plain sight, silently observing
    the virtues of the cool clear water,

Snails and insects scramble up slippery crevices, snakes
    bask, more animals come to satisfy their needs,
The stream rushes on, struggling and forcing its way
    forward.

Joined by another, and another, the swell continues
    until it reaches the big stone bridge,
And is designated as a river.

the bridge by julie pryke

It too flows like beloved water,
    There to offer rest to contemplate the ever-changing view,
    Ebbing and flowing with snake-like vehicles, tortoise cars, ant people,
    Their master, insignificant but mighty, controlling the. passage of so many,
    Restricting their actions.
    Who is the master of the Bridge?
    Mother Nature using a branch to allow her woodland creatures to cross?
    Assisted by 'Green Bridges', protecting wildlife,
    Hedgehogs, badgers,
    deer, foxes,
    wood mice, shrews,
    even frogs and snakes enjoying the safety of these new routes.
    Or is it the man placing his water-smoothed stones in significant order to allow his beloved to cross safely with the precious burden she is carrying?
    The villagers, separated from their fellows?
    The Romans and their armies?
    The industrialists - Brunel, Stevenson, Ford?
    Creators of Spaghetti Junction and the like?

City Dwellers, Country dwellers,

Whitby fishers swinging the bridge, stopping the transition from one side to the other to allow the free passage of their fleet out to the Sea, the master of all, to reap their harvest or inward, to their second life, comradery, family, income, isolation, desolation?

Part of a set of Children's building blocks or made only from rope in precarious situations, the Bridge sees all:

Mountains and Valleys,

Pooh Sticks,

Jumpers

Canal boatmen

Risk-takers,

Thrill seekers.

It allows smooth access to some, transport the priority over people,

Mobility required by all, offered to some.

Practical – yet,

The Bridge is the Key-holder, the passage to all life happenings, between toddler, teen, adult elderly, opening the route to spiritual comfort. A matter of life and death.

the river by julie pryke

The water flows from many streams.
Shimmering, shivering, oh how it gleams.
The streams fuse together, their histories blending,
Weaving their way, seemingly never-ending.
Their identity lost as they run under the bridge,
Twisting and turning over each ridge.

Racing along, they become 'The River',
Pulsing, it celebrates being the life-giver.
Producing large bubbles, steep edges, and ponds.
Homes for small mammals hidden by fronds,
Woodland canopy protecting young life,
But Herons creep in and owls cause much strife.

Children and adults paddle and swim,
Dogs chasing sticks, often jump in.
Thunderstorms filling it, over flood plains,
Houses surrounded; fields submerged again.
Cities for parties in riverside pubs.
Students enjoying their nights and their grub.

Dammed by Beavers, ponds - grounds for trout,
Damned by Companies, letting sewage leak out.
Life dependant on its constant transition,
Industry dependant on its cleansing condition.
Past and present, Environment, Food, Power, Leisure,
Serving all, sustaining all, oft giving pleasure.

Waterfalls created as it drops over cliffs,
Burbling noises, just one of its gifts,
Cascading, pounding, narrow and swift,
Cutting through rocks, making a rift.
Jagged rocks emerge, white water swirls,
Kayaks, Canoes dance with twists, with twirls.

Open land reached and arriving with force,
Water for cattle, for grasses, it weaves a strong course.
Again, through villages, utilizing its power.
A watermill active, producing flour,
Fishermen there displaying their catch,
River cruise trips, there can be no match.

Small spring to giant, it's fulfilled its pledge,
Heads to the sea, the seashore to dredge.
Nearing the coast, rippling, surging,
Achieving its goal, it starts swiftly merging,
Fading, dying, yet arriving with glee,
Reaching its end as it touches the sea.

the sea by julie pryke

The Sea,
Smooth as blue glass.
Kids paddling, laughter,
Building, sandcastles, finding crabs,
Sunshine!

Coach trip,
Visitors arrive, smile,
Amusements, Fish and Chips,
Black clouds, raining, running,
Cafe, Ice.

Waves crash,
Seagulls cry out,
Rocks fall as cliffs crumble,
Coastal storm, erosion, shipwreck,
Lifeboats.

monthly haikus by graham lockwood

A Japanese form of verse consisting of three lines of five, seven and five syllables with an element of time.

January
The fireworks have gone,
The hangover is coming,
Welcome to next year.

February
Hearts soar as the post
Hits the floor, but it is just
The electric bill.

March
In the morning dew
The hares frolicked, chasing does
Into the hedgerows.

April
The morning showers
Cover the daffodils with
Bright sparkling rainbows.

May
First it was Maius,
Then the month of three milkings,
Now there's Star Wars day.

June
Two longest days in
This month of this year, never
To be repeated!

July
Wimbledon is here.
Time to go on holiday.
It's not love at all!

August
'Tis Wakes week, and trains
Are on their way to Brid., from
Dark Satanic Mills.

September
Harvest month to some
And Gerst-monath to others,
 And the Sun flies South.

October
Witches, warlocks and
Monsters walk the Earth this day,
Ended by the Saints.

November
The sunshine strikes the
Soldier's statue in the park.
The crowd falls silent.

December
As the Troikas left,
The snow started to fall and
The lights were soon lost.

Please note that the word 'Maius' is the Roman word for May. The Anglo-Saxons called May 'Thrimicle' which translates as the 'Month of Three Milkings' due to the good grazing available. The Anglo-Saxons called September 'Gerst-monath', which translates as 'Barley month' which they harvested for their favourite drink.

three circular verses
by julie pryke

Great North Run
People, running, Newcastle, September,
September, people, running, Newcastle,
Newcastle, September, people, running,
Running, Newcastle, September, people.

Sometime, Never!
This year, last year, sometime, never,
Never, this year, last year, sometime,
Sometime, never, this year, last year,
Last year, sometime, never, this year.

Scottish Independence Vote
Yes! No! Scotland, vote,
Vote, Yes! No! Scotland,
Scotland, vote, Yes! No!
No! Scotland, vote, Yes!

the misfortunate beck
by tina watkin

It was a shame the bank was robbed.
We each lost all our money.
A culprit must be hunted down
It really wasn't funny.

They put the top man on the job
Setting off with pad in hand
Requesting him to scour the town
And catch the motley band.

For many days the force searched on
But sadly could not find
The money or the culprit
It turned out such a bind.

But then one day a dog rolled up
With something it had found.
Whilst scratching for some old bones
It unearthed from out the ground

A tiny shred of evidence
Buried deep revealed
A button in a swag bag
In a nearby farmer's field.

Inspection of this article
Was clearly quite a shock.
A rookie could confirm
That it belonged to D.S. Beck.

The animal had closed the case
When they'd been in a fog.
The irony of this you see
Solved by the Sergeant's dog.

The team they got together
And admitted they had failed.
Awarded Patch a medal
Whilst D.S. Beck got jailed.

The moral of this story is…
A dog may be your best friend.
But animals are wiser
And truth 'will out' in the end.

bow/bough by julie pryke

He wore a smart bow tie,
And smiled at passersby,
Until he saw 'The one!'

She really looked so good,
He spoke as soon as he could,
Introduced with a great big bow.

She smiled and curtsied back,
As she put down her rucksack,
And straighten the bow in her hair.

Then they both sat down,
With a smile, not a frown,
Under the bough of an old beech tree.

the tree in my front garden by rose johnson

The stalwart tree that stands erect
Proud against a cloudy backdrop
Bows faithfully in my front garden
A sculpted wonder created by time
With arms to encompass life itself
Allowed to live and still not hewn
A breezy giant for feathered friend
Where perches exude from generous girth
Light brown and roughly textured
Encompassed by a feathery spree
Of permanent jade
That sings and sways into the wind
Fragile atop, yet terra firma,
A silent bystander that guards the fore
Whispering caution about the trespass
Amid its wooden realm
Inclining loyal friend that seeks
To brush the pane with true affection.

the fire flower by tina watkin

Spikes are burning on the hills,
Willowherb's afire.
Lighting up the landscape
Is this weeds glowing attire.

Shooting ever taller
 From he cranny in the rock.
Nestled in the hedgerow,
In the field a burning block.

Soon it will transform from
Glowing coat to frothy foam.
These miniature umbrellas
Seeking hard to find a home.

Dusting down the pavement,
As the baker does his dough.
Onward, ever onward
The 'airy-fairies' blow.

The Fire Flower by Tina Watkin

This small invasive army
Is marching boldly on,
But with the gusts of winter
In a moment they are gone.

looter eclipse by rose johnson

When darkness turns the day to night
The triumphant moon bedecks its glittery crown
Feeding upon the ancients fear of doom and gloom
Their dread of harvests wrecked with troubled soul
A daytime moon that mocked their sacrificial rites
With cursed prediction for ill fated times ahead
Punished by the idols of the time
For some iniquitous crime to languish in dire Hades
Secured the time and place of modern solar eclipse
The throng awaits with polymer shades adorned
Amid a gleeful buzz of expectation
To view the phenomena of sun obscured
And loyally watch its five stages
When day becomes a dusky shade
In matter of fact observation
Ill portents dismissed and banished
They see the crown upon its lunar head
But not the sneak thief upon the ground
Who rifles pockets, loots their bags
The eclipse's glory takes its place
And he escapes with all their booty
In portended fate of dire acclaim

tommy : a selection of verse by graham lockwood on the theme of tommy atkins

Tommy Atkins is a slang name for British soldiers that started in the Eighteenth century and is often shortened to just 'Tommy'.

There are several theories of where the name 'Tommy Atkins' originated, and the one that is often quoted is from the Duke of Wellington. In 1794 at the Battle of Boxtel in Flanders, Arthur Wellesley (later The Duke of Wellington) was in command of the 33rd Regiment of Foot and came across a mortally wounded soldier lying in the mud after the battle. His name was Thomas Atkins and the brave soldier told Wellesley "It's all right sir, all in a day's work", just before he died. It is now 1815 and the 'Iron Duke' has defeated Napolean and is asked by the War Office for a name to put in 'The Soldier's Pocket Book' as an example for how the book should be filled out. Thinking back to the Battle of Boxtel, the Duke suggests 'Private Thomas Atkins'.

Please note that the 33rd Regiment of Foot became the Duke of Wellington's Regiment (West Riding), based in Halifax.

haiku

A Japanese form of verse consisting of three lines of five, seven and five syllables with an element of time.

        Tommy's war was quick.
        The first day saw him buried
        Under the Mons' trees.

tanka

Another Japanese form of verse consisting of five, seven, five, seven and seven syllables.

> Tired of fighting in
> Trenches, Tommy joined the Tanks.
> He had his first test,
> And died at Flers on the Somme.
> A Tanka for a Tanker.

limerick

A Limerick is a short, famous poetic form consisting of five lines with a rhyming scheme of AABBA and is often funny and tells a story.

> Tommy Atkins was a wonderful chap,
> After joining, he sat on many a lap.
> He fought for the Frenches,
> Loved all their wenches,
> But all he achieved was the clap.

clerihew

A Clerihew consists of four lines (or several four-line stanzas) with a rhyming scheme AABB and the first line must include the person's name.

> The Commander in Chief was General Haig.
> The results of his plans were known to be vague.
> The Tommys soon learned they were always risky,
> And wished he'd stay at home making cheap Whisky.

palindrome

Palindrome poems are often called 'mirror poems' and are poems that are repeated backwards from halfway through so the first line and the last line are the same, the second line and the second to last line are the same and so on.

> Tommy stood shaking in the British Front Line.
> Over the British parapet
> Through the gapped wire in No-Man's Land
> Dodging the fizz of the bullets whilst artillery sent men
>   to Heaven or Hell
> Through the enemy's wire
> Onto the German parapet
> There are so few of us left, Retreat!
> There are so few of us left, Retreat!
> Onto the German parapet
> Through the enemy's wire
> Dodging the fizz of the bullets whilst artillery sent men
>   to Heaven or Hell
> Through the gapped wire in No-Man's Land
> Over the British parapet
> Tommy stood shaking in the British Front Line

acrostic

The first letter of each sentence spells a name.

Tommy always tried his best.
Over the top with all his Pals,
Mown down in lines by
Machine guns spitting flames.
Young enough to be at school.

All his training couldn't help now, he
Tried his best not to let anyone down.
Killed near the German lines.
In the hot mud he fell
Never to be found.
Serre, 1st July 1916.

-

pangram

A Pangram is a sentence that contains every letter of the alphabet.

Private Tommy Atkins joined the Queen's Own Oxfordshire Hussars on his fourteenth birthday and six months later was killed on the Menin Road and buried alongside his friends in the nearby Zandvoorde Military Cemetery.

six word story

A six-word story is meant to be an entire story in just six words with the reader filling in the blanks.

Tommy enlisted, served, died - still eighteen.

cinquain

A cinquain is a five-line poem consisting of twenty-two syllables: two in the first line, then four, then six, then eight and just two in the last line.

    Listen,
    The guns have stopped.
    I've survived the World War
    Nineteen fourteen to sixteen. No,
    I've died.

shoes by tina watkin

Shoes for comfort, shoes for style
Shoes made for walking
Shoes for sport, shoes for court
Shoes made for stalking.

Shoes with heels, or so it feels.
With backs or just as slip-ons.
Some with laces, some without.
The former you can trip on.

Shoes of canvas, clogs of wood.
Shoes in leather or suede.
Plastic flipflops, satin slippers
 From factory or hand made.

Shoes for wearing every day
Wedged or springy soles.
Shoes discarded in a pile
Now all full of holes.

Shoes by Tina Watkin

Down the street, two left feet
Causing you to wobble,
Make a dash, get out the sash,
Find a shop to cobble.

Or take them to the supermarket
Paired in a bag until
Deposited for recycling
Avoiding the Landfill.

rain by kathryn m. holgate

Standing under the canopy of a very large weeping
    willow tree,
I watch the rain fall as though it's somehow planned its
    route.
I can't pick out the individual raindrops until they hit
    the surface of the water.
I see them now, the circle increases wider and wider
    until they touch.

The sound they make as they drop one by one, is
    replaced by another,
A continuous surprisingly loud sound, that I presumed
    to be repetitive,
But it is not.
It's more the hushed noise of a steam train in the
    station.

Rain by Kathryn M. Holgate

I shelter until the rain stops.
It surprises me how much my ears miss the sound,
But the rain has washed the pavements clean,
And brought out the scent of the roses.

Something new to enjoy!

the halloween cat by matthew holgate

The Halloween Cat
Sat on the mat
Licking his paws
From nice big jaws.

He really enjoyed that fish
Served on a china dish.

It was a treat
The fire gave heat
No tricks tonight
That'll be alright!

rock on, roll on by tina watkin

I wasn't quite alive
Till Carmen Rollers came to town.
The plastic took an age to dry
And often let me down.

But once we went electric,
It almost changed my life
I turned into a 'model'
From a frumpy, dumpy wife.

I'd plug them in and get switched on
Creating curls galore,
Then whisk off down the 'Palais'
And monopolise the floor.

They gave me so much confidence.
It was very clear to see
The 'mouse' sat in the corner
Was indubitably me.

Rock on, Roll On by Tina Watkin

I'd shake my head in rhythm;
Hair cascading round my neck.
I became most uninhibited
Declaring, "What the heck".

The 10p in the meter
Was worth my crowning glory.
For it helped light up my life
And I got that date with Rory.

Without those wax-filled hedgehogs
I'd have been left on the shelf.
But now were called the 'Boogie Duo'
Rory and myself.

We won the cup for Speed Dance
Passing all the other strollers.
Rory said the judged liked his style.
I, credited my rollers.

grenfell by rose johnson

A summer solstice candle breezing midst the twilight air
Where aloft the dizzying height of storey twenty-four
That gazed with envy upon firm Lancaster Green below.

A concrete pitted monument that yearned for the great
    celeste
Brutalist pinnacled cage that cements the scape
Where concrete structures eradicate the green
And take their place betwixt an urban utopia
It couldn't happen again, not after Lakanal
Same thing! An electrical fault on some cheap device
And wrong protocol that caused sad loss of life
So Grenfell Tower had earned its landlords easy money
Their affluence procured from the deprived.

Grenfell by Rose Johnson

The flames played havoc, a creeping plumage that
    consumed new cladding
Where silent souls submitted to the wealth of intense
    heat
Free light for rich Chelsea and Kensington to peruse
Across the great divide of worth
To witness this sacrificial rite of greed
One exit to free them from their plight
Secured within this night-time prison
Where embers from the debris punctured the sky
And fell like tears upon the deep below
As the blaze took hold with vengeance square
Who knows the fear behind those walls
Of those who faced a fate within this burning pyre
Stuck in the lofty heights of concrete block
Where dwelling upon dwelling saves space
And claustrophobia abounds

Charred shrine upon the sky-line grey
Sad recall for those who remain
There but for providence go....
The night that

also by denholme scribes

A Collection of Our Scribblings, May 2022
Some Christmas Scribblings, November 2022
Scribbling Again, October 2023

about the authors

The Denholme Scribes come together every Tuesday morning to share our latest literary efforts, discuss ideas, and support each other. Coffee and cakes set the stage, and experienced writers and newcomers alike are welcome.

Each member brings their own ideas, genres, and styles. Whether it's evocative poetry, short stories, or personal essays that offer glimpses into lived experiences, the Denholme Scribes embrace the power of storytelling in all its forms.

Every year we publish a collection of our poems and prose. This, our latest anthology of verse, is a celebration of our dedication and hard work throughout the year.

You need look no further if you want a cracking Christmas present for your friends and families.

Enjoy!